MW01291995

ENDORSEMENTS

"This marvelous little devotional book teaches us about God's principles for our lives through the stories of the outdoors and God's creatures. It is amazing how Stan Lake has taken the lessons of life expressed in and through animals, insects, and nature to show with scripture the truth of God's creation. I met Stan when he was a student with us at the *Vision for Evangelism for the Next Generation* weekend at the Billy Graham Library. His heart is truly that others might know the One who created all. Stan uses nature and the Creator 's words to share creative devotions to build His Kingdom."

Tom Phillips
Vice President, Billy Graham Evangelistic Association
Billy Graham Library

"Stan Lake, clearly loves God and His marvelous creation. This is evident from the many great examples from nature that Stan uses to illustrate Kingdom principles and encourage all to follow Christ.

I highly recommend "Whispers' in the Woods".

John R. Berry (Rev)
Herpetologist, author & speaker.

"Stan has a great heart for God and His creation so it's awesome to see him combine his passions to write this fun and inspiring book! Read it by yourself or with your children- it will be a great way to grow closer to God and appreciate what He made!"

Joe Wyrostek
Apostolic Elder
Metro Praise International Church
Chicago, IL.
www.mpichurch.org

“Nature is always a great teacher when you stop and study it. Stan Lake has shared his revelations from nature and God’s word combining them to be truly thought provoking. Stan is a voice crying from and for the wilderness to help us make our ways straight with the Lord’s help.”

Richard Norris DVM MBA
Founder of Leading Men Only
Perth, Scotland

“Stan Lake finds thoughts and messages from the creation he catches and releases those truths to his audience. All ages will enjoy reading the stories and experience personal growth as Stan finds the supernatural contained in the nature around us all.”

Dr. Mike Rakes
Lead Pastor, WinstonSalemFirst
Winston Salem, NC

“If you have a love for our creator God and his handiwork then this devotional from Stan Lake highlights in a humorous and relevant way the constant inspiration that surrounds us and can be drawn from in our daily lives. Stan takes the everyday ignored aspects of creation and applies them to sound biblical teaching that we can all use to develop our walk with God.

As someone who prefers to worship God in his creation I can draw a lot of parallels from Stan’s teaching and appreciate the truth he reveals through the masters work. Whispers In The Woods will encourage you to pause, value and thank God for all he has done.”

Clinton Kirkpatrick.
Believers Bushcraft
County Antrim, Northern Ireland.

"Stan has given us a rare and insightful look both at nature and our Christian walk. Be encouraged as you journey with him."

Dr. Stephen Lee Carter,MD
Cincinatti, Ohio

As metropolis turns to megalopolis we may lose sight of God's creation unless we look up, and the sounds of the city can distract unless we're otherwise distracted by the feed through our ear buds. For those desiring some genuine quiet time, away from the city hustle, away from car alarms, sirens and jackhammers, there is "Whispers in the Woods".

Take this opportunity to go green and a multitude of colors to start your week or escape in the middle, outside the city with Stan Lake's "Whisper in the Woods", and realize the blessings through Christ Jesus that Paul wrote about in Ephesians 1:10, "as a plan for the fullness of time, to unite all things in Him, things in heaven and things on earth."

Stephen Wilber
Aliso Viejo, CA

"It is with great pleasure I highly recommend STAN LAKE's wonderful book, WHISPERS in the WOODS! He found me through social media, gave a 'whisper' in the dark, and as fate would have it, through his persistence and my time availability, I was able to read it. I was thoroughly expecting a very worthy but 'holier than thou' approach- boy was I ever wrong! Stan has captured the most wonderful Essence of Nature and the Great Spirit in a way that connects us too our roots and Mother Earth, while touching our hearts and spirits with kind and wise words that refresh, nourish and tickle all at the same time. That is no small accomplishment. I am sure Stan would say, he had a guiding hand! If you need something to fill a dark space in your life, this enjoyable and easy read is like a cool drink of fresh water in the desert. This book brought me great joy!"

Mykel Hawke
Retired Special Forces Officer, Military & Contractor Combat Veteran, TV Host & Producer, Author, Designer, Black Belt and Family Counselor.

Whispers in the Woods

AN INVITATION TO EXPERIENCE THE WONDER OF GOD'S CREATION

STAN LAKE

www.CatchingCreation.com

Editing by Allonda Hawkins
Formatting by Allen Vesterfelt

Photo Credit:
Derek Cook - pg 3, 13, 27, 31. 53, 100
Chance Feimster - pg 5, 9, 24, 28, 32, 39, 40, 43, 44, 56, 64, 84, 96
Andrea O'Connell - pg 6
Stan Lake - pg 10, 14, 51, 71
Chad Hall - pg 17, 20
John Mayer - pg 18
John Tann - pg 21
ikewinski - pg 23
Brett McBain - pg 35
Finch Lake - pg 36
Jim Bauer - pg 47
Neil Conway - pg 48
Kimberly Robyn - pg 52
Kostas Krev - pg 55
Kev Chapman - pg 59
Jyrki Salmi - pg 60
Berit Watkin - pg 67
Patrick Feller - pg 68
Filipe Fortes - pg 72
Tambako - pg 75
Carl Koch - pg 76
Bob Ellis - pg 79
Clinton Steeds - pg 80
Linda Tanner - pg 83
Jay Erickson - pg 87
Don McCullough - pg 88
David Denis - pg 89
Steven LaVine - pg 91, 99
William Warby - pg 92
Geoffry Gallaway - pg 95
Rasmus Bøgeskov Larsen - pg 98

CONTENTS

ACKNOWLEDGMENTS

A special thanks to my wife Jessica for allowing me to turn our home into a zoo and for putting up with my constant muddy boots, wet socks, and endless trips to wild places. Thanks to my Grandmother for teaching me the beauty of nature and helping me to develop a strong desire for books and writing at an early age. To my Mother for always supporting my endless ventures from punk rock bands as a teen to collecting reptiles as a child (and adult). Thanks to my Dad for countless hours spent outdoors fishing, splitting wood and my love for flannel and eggnog. Thanks to Shawn and Staci for always being my partners in crime and co-adventurers as kids in the wilds of North Carolina. To Mike for taking me camping as a kid and modeling true manhood for me. To Anne for modeling what a true believer in Christ looks like. To Daniel for telling me about Jesus while we were in Iraq together and walking with me after we got home, leading me to Christ and founding Catching Creation with me. Thanks to the McGee's for your endless love and support. Thanks to everyone else who has been a part of my life and ministry, there are too many of you to thank and know that your influence on my life is invaluable and I owe it all to all of you!

FORWARD

What a privilege to be asked to participate in this great devotional package. Why the term "package"...the passion for truth reflected in the life of my good friend, Stan. A lover of God and mankind but equally amazed by the entirety of God's Creation.

An experiential worshiper, who married into a family known for their artistic talents, he respects the tradition of worship while engaging the most outlandish expressions of faith among humans.

Still yet he finds his place of reverence with the lesser of creation. Whether reptiles, the most misunderstood of all creatures, toads or tall trees, Stan recognizes the validity of their praise to God. Be it vibrant color, vocal croaks or waiving branches, to Stan, they all reflect His glory. Sing with melody in your heart as you enjoy or possibly even shrink back with caution at this man's courageous pursuit of his Lord, as he, Catches Creation.

John R Bost, Mayor
Village of Clemmons, NC
President, Master Counsel & Associates, Inc

INTRODUCTION

From the earliest moment I can remember, I have been fascinated with animals and everything that grows and lives outdoors. The siren song of the wilderness has drawn me into its wild arms time and time again. I have found such solace over the years in the woods that I just can't shake its beckoning for me to return home. My earliest memory of God was in his creation and His voice would guide me to discover His created things. Looking back I am thankful for the alone times I spent as a kid, with my child like faith, just walking in wonder in the woods.

Show and tell in elementary school was always some animal that I had rescued from its home in the woods and gave it freedom by placing it in my aquarium. I cannot tell you how many fowler's toads, fence lizards, or box turtles I kept against their will in my room as a child. My love of animals seemed to grow as I did. I remember being told when I was in high school by a relative that I needed to grow up and stop playing in the creek - I pray I never do. It seems the older I get the more I am drawn to the wild and the busier I get the more I miss the simplicity held within mossy trees and muddy banks.

My education of God's creation was through his ever present whispering into my life while I took these lonely walks through his intricately designed masterpiece. I have no idea how I know where to look for animals or how exactly I find them, other than just listening to the gentle whispering of the Creator. I know this may sound crazy but it is true and the best part is with each new discovery, God reveals more of Himself through His creation. During the course of this short book I hope these 52 devotionals speak to you. My prayer is that you are able to experience the wonder of God's creation and above all else fall deeper in love with the Creator of the universe.

Job 12:7-10

"But ask the animals, and they will teach you, or the birds of the air, and they will tell you; or speak to the earth, and it will teach you, or let the fish of the sea inform you. Which of all these does not know that the hand of the L*ORD* has done this? *In his hand is the life of every creature and the breath of all mankind."*

ARE YOU HIDING IN THE GARDEN?

Have you ever done something so hideous that you just wanted to hide from everyone and everything, including God? In the book of Genesis, chapter 3 to be specific, Adam and Eve did that very thing. They were instructed not to eat the fruit from the tree of knowledge of good and evil, but after a crafty deception by a serpent with the gift of gab, they found themselves disobeying a direct order from God. What do the creation duo do next?

They do the only sensible thing in their minds; they hide from God in the fear and shame of their sinfulness. This is illustrated in Genesis 3:8-10 *"Then the man and his wife heard the sound of the Lord God as he was walking in the garden in the cool of the day, and they hid from the Lord God among the trees of the garden. But the Lord God called to the man, 'Where are you?' He answered, "I heard you in the garden, and I was afraid because I was naked; so I hid."*

I notice several things in these short few verses that speak volumes to the love of our heavenly Father. The first thing I notice is that despite our shame and sinfulness, God still looks for us where we are hiding. God is God, He knew exactly what Adam and Eve had done and where they were hiding and He still pursued them.

Adam and Eve hid among the very thing that caused them to sin in the first place, they hid "among the trees in the garden" and God went where they were. Lastly God knew they were naked the whole time and didn't fault them for the things they lacked in knowledge (and in this case clothing). He loved them enough to look for them in their state of shame. Are you hiding in the garden?

God is still God and He knows that you are naked; He knows you are scared and because of your sinfulness you feel unworthy of having a relationship with Him. There is good news! You are unworthy of God and your sin does separate you from Him, but He has made a way for you through His son Jesus Christ. Just like God pursued our first parents in the beginning He is also pursuing you, even in your nakedness.

In Genesis 3:21 God sacrifices an animal to cover our sins and nakedness and gives the animal skins to Adam and Eve to cover up. From the beginning there always had to be innocent bloodshed to cover our deficiency, our sin. God did this once and for all in the pure and spotless lamb of Jesus Christ, His only son. God knows your nakedness and he has prepared a way for you to cover your shame by the blood of Jesus. Will you accept his free gift? Will you come out of hiding or are you going to stay hidden among the trees in the garden?

ARE YOU LIKE THE TREE PLANTED BY WATER?

One of my favorite trees in the forest happens to be a small obscure tree called the ironwood, sometimes called the blue beech. This tree lives out its life very close to streams and in areas where the soil stays moist continually. The ironwood is known for its strength and when you touch its trunk it feels twisted like someone flexing their muscles. This tree is a very real reminder of what the Psalmist is saying in the first Psalm.

Psalm 1:3 says, *"He is like a tree planted by streams of water, which yields its fruit in season and whose leaf does not wither. Whatever he does prospers."* When we are walking in the righteousness of God we are in an environment that is nurturing to our soul and allows us to put down deep roots that are sustained by God. We will bear fruit in the proper season and are able to reap the rewards of our faith because our God is faithful. Are you like the tree planted by water?

WOULD YOU DRINK FROM A BIRDBATH?

Have you ever watched a bird joyfully roll around in a birdbath after a summer rain? It is quite the experience. The bird seems to not have a care in the world and almost seems to enjoy its soak. Birds will use anything from a shallow puddle to a store-bought birdbath from your local hardware store. As long as it has water in it they will utilize it. A birdbath will be filled every time it rains or an attentive birdwatcher fills the bath. The water just sits there in the reservoir, constantly being refilled but never flowing out. This leads to stagnation and some of the nastiest water one can imagine.

Jesus says in John 7:38 " *"Whoever believes in me, as the Scripture has said, streams of living water will flow from within him."* How many times as believers in Jesus do we just want to be like the birdbath and constantly just filled, filled, filled to boost up our own spirit? The nature of being a true believer is more like the stream. The spirit lives in us and flows through us. A stream is constant, both being filled and being poured out, unlike the birdbath. To a world dying for something fresh and life giving to drink, we as believers should be offering water from streams of living water and not being so self-centered that we only care about filling our personal birdbath. Would you drink from a birdbath?

DO YOU GIVE GOOD GIFTS?

Have you ever received a gift that you didn't ask for but you are thankful for nonetheless? I always chuckle when I read scriptures like Luke 11:11 which says, *"Which of you fathers, if your son asks for a fish, will give him a snake instead?"* Even though I understand the context of the verse as it is talking about prayer and how much our heavenly Father loves us and will give us good gifts, I can't help but think of my own father and the gift I got one Christmas as a kid. I don't remember asking my dad for a tarantula; actually I think it probably wasn't anywhere near my Christmas list. Still, my dad knew I loved animals and so next to my toy crossbow was a mini terrarium with a bow and a large hairy spider in it. I have to admit I was terrified of the tarantula but I wanted to make my dad proud and take care of my newly acquired arachnid friend.

Scripture says that even though we are evil we still know how to give good gifts and it encourages us to seek our heavenly Father because He will give us abundantly more than we could even ask. God has given us the greatest gift in all of humanity by sending His son, Jesus Christ, to Earth for our salvation. My father got me the tarantula out of the goodness of his heart and that to him was a good gift. There was no malice involved and yet it wasn't exactly what I wanted, but as we seek the Lord He will give us what we truly desire as we confide in Him and submit to His will. Once we align ourselves with God and determine ourselves to seek Him and His righteousness we will be astounded at the "good gifts" our heavenly Father bestows on us! Do you give good gifts?

ARE YOU ON THE RIGHT PATH?

Have you ever heard the statement "all paths lead to God?" I was recently hiking at a place I had not previously hiked before and realized I didn't know which path actually led to the place I wanted to go. If I used the logic that all paths would lead me to the goal I set out to find, I can only imagine where I would end up. The problem with that statement is that all paths eventually do lead to God, but all paths don't allow you to stay in His presence. We will all be judged for the actions and choices we make in this life and we will all eventually meet the Creator of the universe, so in that regard I can agree that all paths lead to God. The problem is however, if we don't accept Jesus and are cleaned of our sins by his blood, God's justice will send us to eternal punishment.

Jesus says in John 14:6, *"I am the way and the truth and the life. No one comes to the Father except through me."* God has given us a way out, a way to the right path, through His son Jesus Christ. We have the opportunity in this life to be forgiven and placed back in right standing with God if we accept the sacrifice of His son. If you're seeking to find the right path and don't want to just be lost in the woods, I encourage you to look to Jesus. He is the way, the only way! Are you on the right path?

HAS SOMEONE LITTERED YOUR VIEW OF GOD?

I will often go hiking deep into the woods with the hopes of finding some new spot untainted by the hand of man. I am continually astonished to find that every new secret hard to find spot that I discover is littered with beer cans and old tires and any number of other forms of litter. It amazes me the lengths people will go to discard washing machines and old vehicles or simply the spots people decide to throw away any conceivable thing imaginable. If I took the popular view of most people regarding our God and compared bad experiences with the church to litter in the woods, you could say it's the wilderness' fault that all the litter exists. However, we know that would be the furthest thing from the truth.

It's not God's fault you have had a bad experience with church or even other believers in Christ. The heart of the issue is simply bad decisions made by people. Even though Christians are followers of Jesus and should subscribe to all of His teachings, we often miss the mark and can litter the views of unbelievers and believers alike.

In Paul's epistle to the Philippians he illustrates this point in chapter 2:1-4 *"If you have any encouragement from being united with Christ, if any comfort from his love, if any fellowship with the Spirit, if any tenderness and compassion, then make my joy complete by being like-minded, having the same love, being one in spirit and purpose. Do nothing out of selfish ambition or vain conceit, but in humility consider others better than yourselves. Each of you should look not only to your own interests, but also to the interests of others."* If we can remember these words from the Apostle Paul we can help others see the true beauty of Christ's church and truly reflect the nature of Jesus to a world that so desperately needs to see something genuine and uncontaminated. Has someone littered your view of God?

ARE YOU LIKE A HOLLOW TREE?

Every time I see a hollow tree while hiking through the woods I always knock on it in hopes of seeing some sleepy animal coming out to greet me. There have been a few occasions where my habitual knocking have produced something wild, like the time I found a nest of baby raccoons and the time a swarm of angry bees erupted from the cavity. It's not always a good experience initially, but the mystery of the tree's cavity always gets the best of me.

A rotting of the heartwood in the tree typically causes hollows in trees. This can occur as a result of stress brought on by disease, lightening strikes, fungi, bacteria and a slew of other agitators. The emptiness in these trees weakens them and can lead to their death if the cavity is great enough. The integrity of the tree is compromised because the strength of the tree lies in its core. The rotted heartwood negates its structural integrity making it susceptible to breaking during storms. We can use this as an obvious parallel if we allow the stress of this world to cause emptiness in us. When we are stressed out and we allow emptiness to consume us, any number of things can fill the void.

Proverbs 4:23 says, *"Above all else, guard your heart, for it is the wellspring of life."* As believers in Christ, we are called to guard our hearts because that is where Jesus takes residence as we believe in Him. Our heart is the wellspring of our lives and out of the excess of our heart we will speak as scripture says. As believers we can fill our emptiness with the love of Christ because He is more than enough to satisfy our every need! Are you like a hollow tree?

WHAT'S THAT WRITING SPIDER TRYING TO SAY?

Writing spiders have always been somewhat of an autumn fascination of mine. Ever since I was a kid I have always enjoyed spying on their plump yellow and black bodies clinging to their sticky webs. My grandmother's garden and flowerbeds have always been prime real estate for my arachnid friends. They have always indicated a closing of one season and a reminder of cooler days to come. The zigzag "writing" found in their webs have also always intrigued me. What is this stigmatized animal trying to say, I have often wondered.

When I look at this animal through the lens of scripture it's easy enough for me to see Christ in even the most offensive of God's creation, the spider. Jeremiah 51:15 says *"He made the earth by His power; He founded the world by His wisdom and stretched out the heavens by His understanding."* The writing spider is sometimes called the "St. Andrew's Cross Spider" because of the way it pairs its legs and appears to be in the shape of a cross. The zigzag pattern of X's in the web draws your attention immediately and brings the focus to the cross. As the Apostle Paul says in Romans 1:20, we are without excuse because the glory of God is all around us. We just have to open our eyes.

ARE YOU TIRED OF FLYING SOLO?

Have you ever been struck with awe as a group of geese fly above you in their clamorous V formation? Seeing this phenomenon has always been a delight for me for as long as I can remember. The geese fly this particular way when they migrate south because it helps them to not get exhausted flying such far distances.

Romans 12:3-5 says, *"For by the grace given me I say to every one of you: Do not think of yourself more highly than you ought, but rather think of yourself with sober judgment, in accordance with the faith God has distributed to each of you.* ***4*** *For just as each of us has one body with many members, and these members do not all have the same function,* ***5*** *so in Christ we, though many, form one body, and each member belongs to all the others."*

The geese function as a team, not as individuals, just as we are supposed to operate. If the same geese flew south individually they would take much longer to get there and could potentially die because of the stress involved in flying alone. The function of the V formation is to provide less wind resistance for the group, thus making it easier to fly in tandem. When the leader of the group gets tired he can fall back to the rear of the formation and essentially draft with the others as they all fly as a unit. This V formation also requires each goose behind the leader to keep the others in its direct line of sight so they are all accountable to one another. If one is suffering or falls back they're even able to adjust their flight to accommodate the individual in need.

Jesus has called us as believers to live in community. We are not set apart to become lone rangers but to live in unity with one another, holding each other accountable and sharing in the gifts he has blessed each of us with. We all aren't good at the same things but thankfully as a collective we can achieve the purposes of Christ by combining our talents together. Are you tired of flying solo?

DO YOU HAVE WISDOM LIKE AN OWL?

Have you ever heard the saying "wise like an owl?" The personification of the owl seems to suggest that they have an inherent wisdom that we humans may or may not possess. The truth is, an owl is no wiser than a crow or hawk or any other large predatory bird and surely not wiser than a human being. This idiom probably has to do with the way an owl looks very serious and almost seems to be contemplatively listening as it sits silently in the trees.

The good news is that our Lord gives wisdom generously to those who ask. James 1:5 says *"If any of you lacks wisdom, he should ask God, who gives generously to all without finding fault, and it will be given to him."* Proverbs 2:6 says, *"For the LORD gives wisdom, and from his mouth come knowledge and understanding."* If you truly want to be wise, look not to the owl but to the God who created owls! Do you have wisdom like an owl?

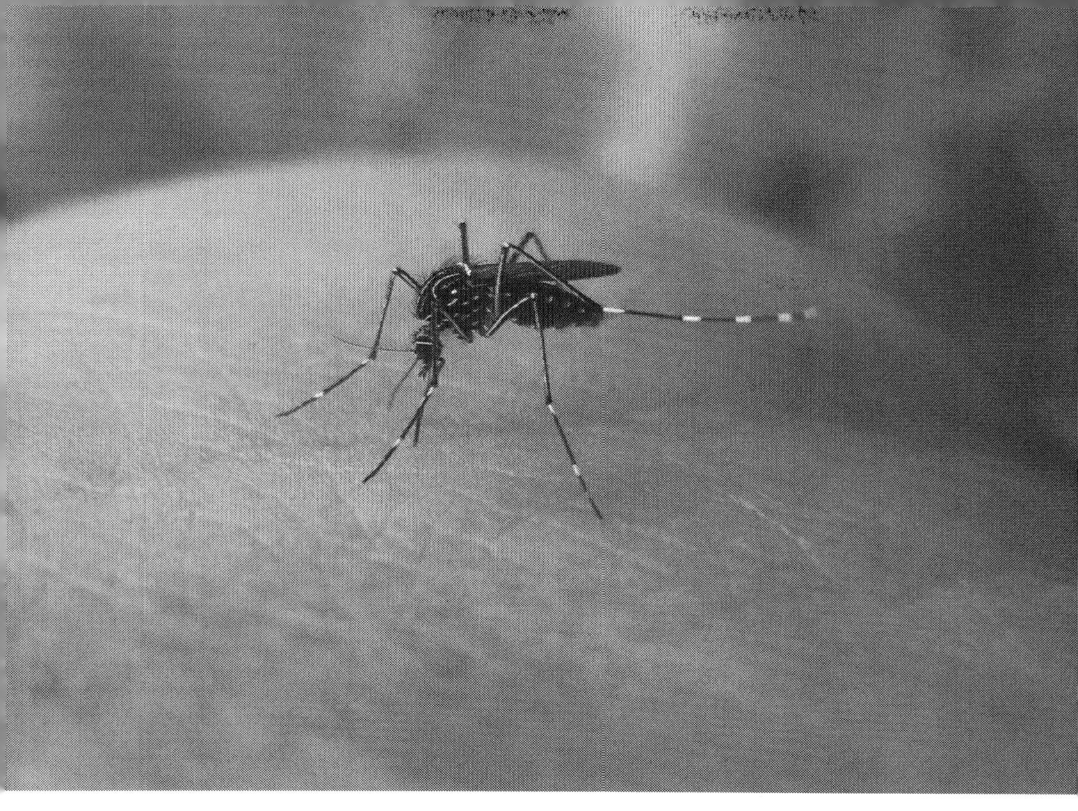

DO YOU BUZZ LIKE A MOSQUITO?

Have you ever felt that annoying buzz of a mosquito around your ears that could only symbolize an itching fit later? They seem to serve as a warning for things to come and mostly a warning of potential discomfort. How many times do we as Christians buzz around people who find us annoying, only to be uncomfortable later when the gospel message isn't fully received.

A mosquito brings life to those smart enough to feed on them. Bats, tadpoles, small lizards and a slew of other organisms see the mosquito in a much different light than we do. Just like the person, who needs to be fed the buzz of the real Gospel, needs that life giving sustenance. So even though a mosquito is annoying to most and often gets swatted, it has a purpose and so do you. *"He said to them, "Go into all the world and preach the gospel to all creation."* Mark 16:15. Jesus commands us to preach his good news to all creation. It's not a suggestion, so let's get buzzing about the kings business!

DO YOU CARRY THE LIGHT INSIDE OF YOU?

As believers in Christ we are called to be the light of the world like it speaks of in Matthew 5:14-16. If Christ is in fact inside of us then we should proclaim his name and let that light shine in this dark world. Look at the firefly, or as we call them in the south, lightening bugs.

They are set apart and different from other insects because they, like Christ followers, carry the light inside of them. So as summer darkness creeps in you can see the flashing beauty of these tiny bugs. Amid the blackness there is light. No matter how dark it is outside, when these little guys flash, it illuminates the darkness.

That is how we as Christians should be in this dark world. Our individual lights for Christ may be the only things shining out amid the darkness that surrounds us. So when you see these little light wielding creations give thanks to God for the light he has bestowed upon us as believers and let that light shine for him.

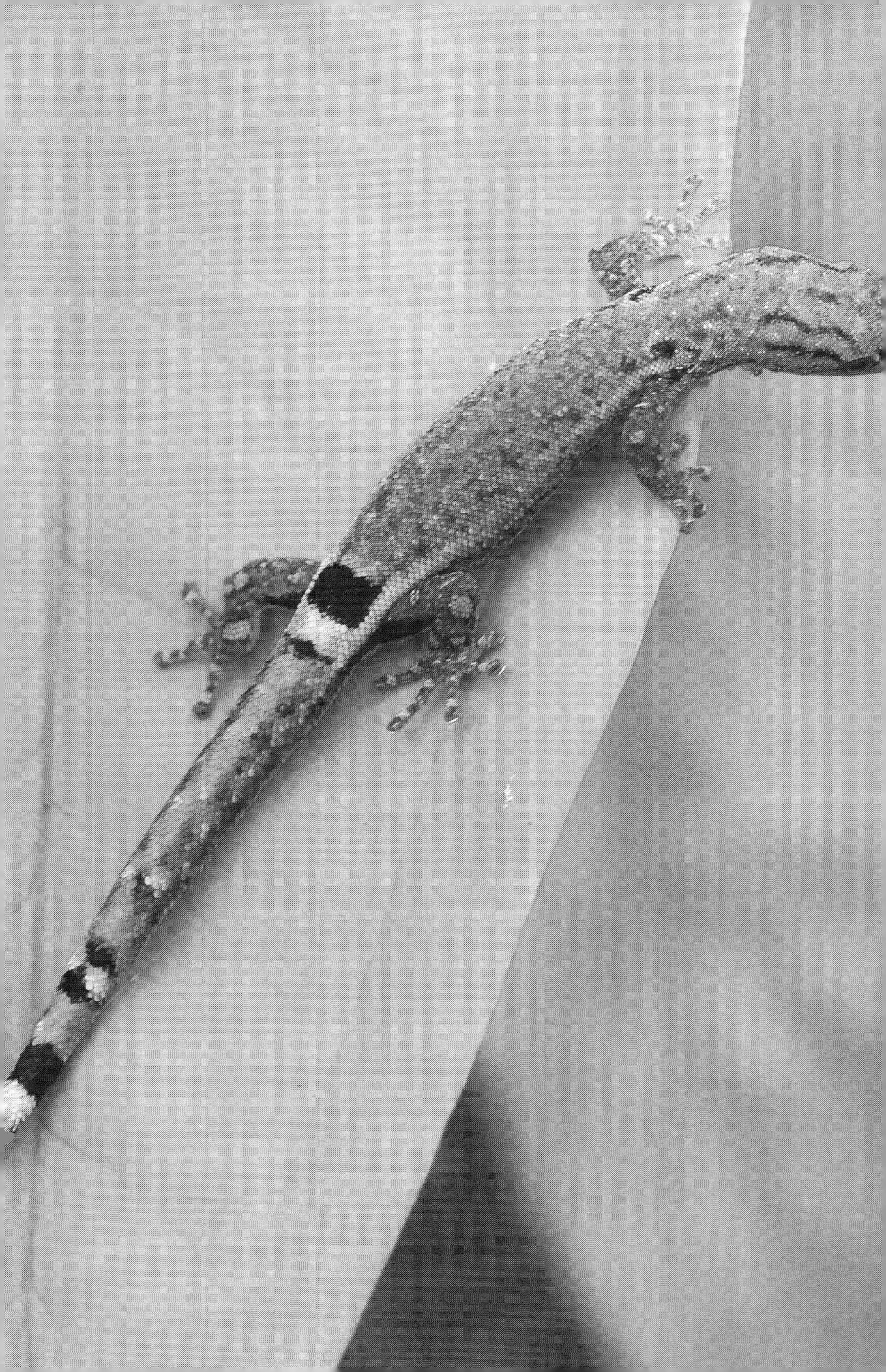

A LIZARD CAN BE REGENERATED, CAN YOU?

I had the privilege of growing up in the country and spending most of my time outside catching snakes, frogs, lizards and just about anything else that crawls. One thing I learned from a very early age was that if you grabbed a lizard by the tail in an attempt to catch it, you would be left with a bloody wiggling appendage. Lizards have fracture planes in their tails that help them to drop their tails in an effort to entice and distract a predator so it can make a quick escape. The coolest part of the whole process is that not only does the lizard drop its tail but also the tail regenerates eventually and grows back.

Ezekiel 36:26 says *"I will give you a new heart and put a new spirit in you; I will remove from you your heart of stone and give you a heart of flesh."* The Lord allows our hearts to be regenerated by accepting Jesus, and the coolest part is that the heart he gives us as we accept him is one that will function much better than the one before. Ezekiel says that before the Lord gives us a new heart and spirit, it is like we have a heart of stone. When Jesus enters and regenerates our heart he makes us into a new creation and changes our nature from one that is more like a cold stone to that of a warm heart ready to love. Next time you see a lizard with a stub tail remember that just as his tail will eventually grow back and regenerate, Jesus is doing that same work in your heart as we learn to follow and obey His commands. A lizard can be regenerated, can you?

ARE YOU OBEDIENT LIKE A DOG?

If you have ever spent time with a well-trained and good-natured dog you can understand the joy they bring to us in their obedience. The situation seems to be quite the opposite when you encounter a dog that is lacking in proper training. The same is true for human beings. When we make a profession of faith but lack obedience to Christ it creates an atmosphere similar to the wild dog. People tend to remember the crazy behavior and abrasive experience and it takes quite a while to repair the damage of disobedience.

2 John 1:6 says, "*And this is love: that we walk in obedience to his commands. As you have heard from the beginning, his command is that you walk in love.*" When we walk in obedience to Christ and follow His commands we are truly showing the love that He demands of us. When we truly understand the teachings of Jesus and are obedient to them, we can genuinely walk in truth with the love of Christ. Are you obedient like a dog?

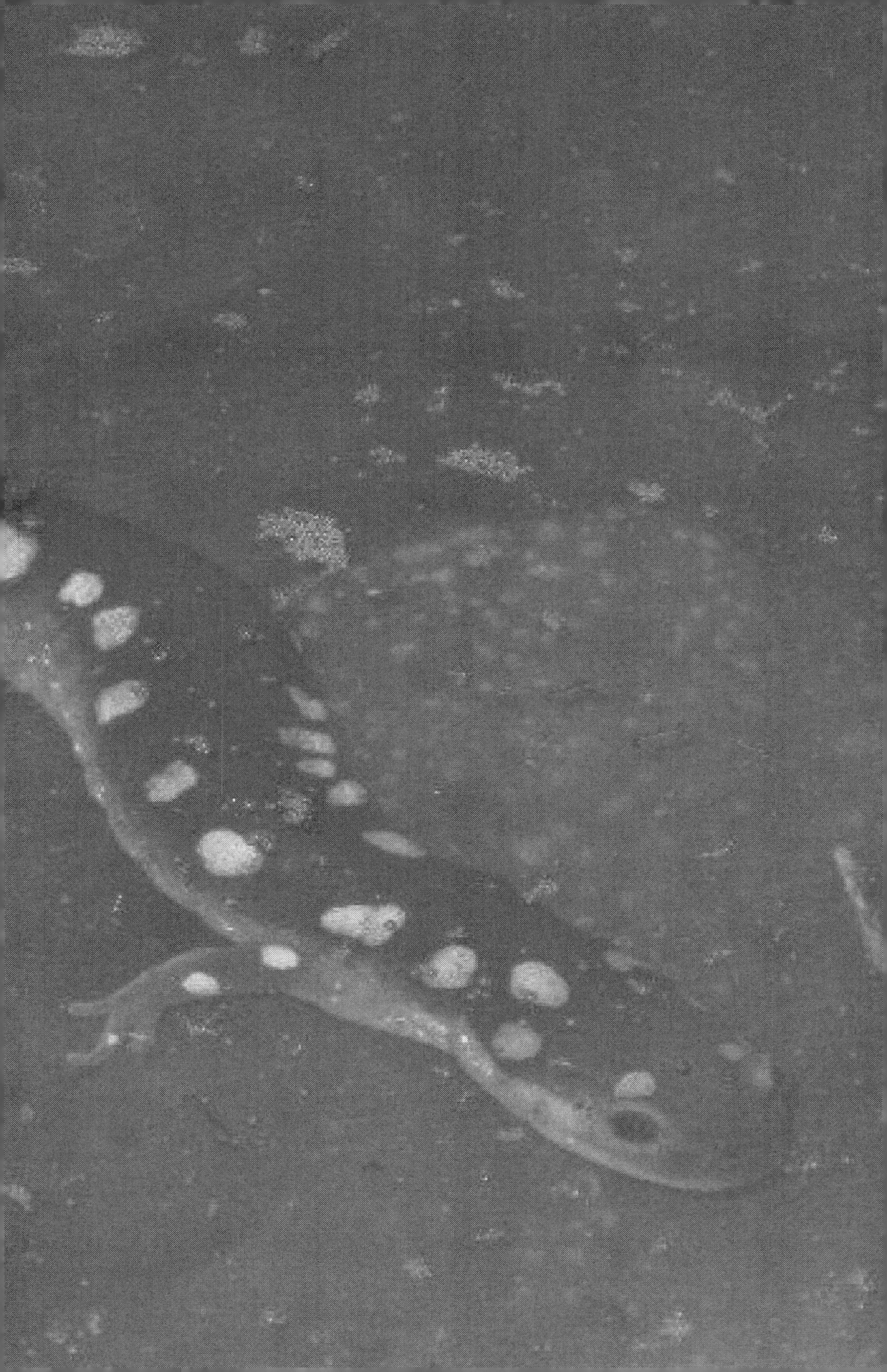

DO CONDITIONS HAVE TO BE PERFECT FOR YOU TO COME OUT?

Several years ago I had the amazing opportunity to see spotted salamanders breeding. I know what you're thinking, but I promise it's not gross. The salamanders look as if they are all dancing underwater and you see flashes of bluish black with speckles of yellow and white spots glimmering in the moonlight. The conditions required to get spotted salamanders out en mass to breed need to be almost perfect. The vernal (or temporary) pools that they lay their eggs in have to be the correct depth and PH, the humidity and temperature have to be just right and it typically follows a heavy rain. Once their annual "dance" is complete they go back to their subterranean burrows and are rarely seen again until the next breeding season.

Hebrews 10:24-25 says, *"And let us consider how we may spur one another on toward love and good deeds.* ***25*** *Let us not give up meeting together, as some are in the habit of doing, but let us encourage one another—and all the more as you see the Day approaching."* The writer of Hebrews is encouraging us to not only love one another and do good works but to also not forger the purpose for meeting. We don't just go to church to keep up appearances, at least I hope not!

The real reason we assemble together is to mutually encourage one another so that we can do the work of the ministry that we ALL are called to do. The Lord has given us all specific gifts which we are to use to help edify the body and grow the kingdom of God. We meet together so as to help one another from falling by the wayside or getting discouraged and giving up. Do conditions have to be perfect for you to come out?

AN ELEPHANT NEVER FORGETS, DO YOU?

Have you ever heard the phrase "an elephant never forgets?" Are we to believe that an elephant literally never forgets? Heavens no! The phrase seems to coincide with the fact that elephants will follow the same pathways and ancestral routes to watering holes and even elephant burial sites. It seems as if they are hardwired to remember and will stop at nothing to follow the path they have always followed, even if that means trampling a newly constructed village that just happens to be in their way.

Isaiah 43:18-19 says, *"Forget the former things; do not dwell on the past. See, I am doing a new thing! Now it springs up; do you not perceive it? I am making a way in the desert and streams in the wasteland.* When we accept Jesus he makes us into a new thing completely and even though we can't completely forget our past we can certainly choose not to dwell on it.

Unlike the elephants we can choose to divert our pathways and not go down the same old roads of sin that we have gone down for generations. Doesn't joy spring up in you when you think about the wasteland that your heart used to be, but because of Christ, streams of living water now flow from within you? When I think about it in that context it's easy for me to forget about my former life and be glad in the person Christ is making me. I don't have to wander down those old paths! An elephant never forgets, do you?

DO YOU PRAY LIKE A MANTIS?

Have you ever looked at a praying mantis up close and thought to yourself "wow this creature looks to be the basis for all of Hollywood's alien movies?" They are called praying mantis because it appears they are "praying" due to the posture of their arms when they are poised to strike. I find it quite interesting that we often equate them to prayer just simply based on looks, similar to the Pharisees in the New Testament, as they would stand on street corners and pray aloud to look more righteous than the average person. The truth is, a praying mantis doesn't pray and even more graphically after they put on their appearance of righteousness they go home and bite the head off of their mate.

Matthew 6:5 says, *"And when you pray, do not be like the hypocrites, for they love to pray standing in the synagogues and on the street corners to be seen by men. I tell you the truth, they have received their reward in full."* Jesus wants us to genuinely pray and seek him in private. We don't need to put on a show so that other people think we are righteous. The purpose of our prayers is to establish a personal relationship with Jesus Christ and to communicate with the creator of the universe.

So a praying mantis appears to be religious and appears to be holy but then behind closed doors they aren't so friendly to their loved ones. This shouldn't be! True prayer will draw us not only closer to Jesus but to those around us. We will begin to take on his likeness and characteristics through our obedience in prayer. Do you pray like a mantis?

HAVE YOU BEEN REDEEMED LIKE A SHELTER PET?

Several years ago I visited a local animal shelter with the intention of finding a dog to take home with me. I had a very specific dog in mind and scoured the Internet to see if any were available on the shelter's website. I found the breed I was looking for and decided to go check it out. When I got to the shelter the dog I came to see was as disinterested in me as an animal could be. It wasn't really the dog I had in mind either, and I was looking for something quite specific. My intention was to find a boxer that was full blooded and that had a white coat. After I put the disinterested mix-breed dog back into its kennel a friend of mine came around the corner with the perfect dog. I immediately fell in love with him and have him to this day. He was the most energetic and loving white boxer I had ever seen and we hit it off immediately. This animal knew that he had been bought with a price and paid me back in his love and loyalty to me.

Did you know that Jesus Christ bought you with a price? Isaiah 44:22 says *I have swept away your offenses like a cloud, your sins like the morning mist. Return to me, for I have redeemed you.* I don't know what caused my furry friend to end up in the shelter, but had I not intervened and redeemed him, his future would have certainly ended in his untimely demise. The same is true for us as followers of Jesus Christ. Had Jesus not stepped into history and intervened on our behalf redeeming us from our sins, we would most certainly die in our sins. Jesus purchases us with a price, redeems us and we are required to pay him back with our loyalty, devotion, love and obedience. Just like with my dog, this isn't a hard thing when you know your master loves you and chose you specifically. Have you been redeemed like a shelter pet?

DO YOU CREATE A SUITABLE ENVIRONMENT FOR OTHERS?

Have you ever had the opportunity to witness beavers creating their dams in a wetland habitat? It is quite an amazing phenomenon to experience. A beaver can create an entirely new habitat in a very short time. They are very hard working animals and by their diligence and boldness they are able to gnaw through trees and divert the flow of water in fresh water ecosystems. They have the ability to literally change the course of streams and creeks and to use their dams to create ponds and swamps. They change the entire topography and by doing so they create a new ecosystem that can support a variety of animals that previously couldn't have lived in the area. In many cases their habitat transformation can be a blessing to other wildlife by providing new homes and places to forage for food.

1 Thessalonians 5:12-15 says, *"Now we ask you, brothers, to respect those who work hard among you, who are over you in the Lord and who admonish you. Hold them in the highest regard in love because of their work. Live in peace with each other. And we urge you, brothers, warn those who are idle, encourage the timid, help the weak, be patient with everyone. Make sure that nobody pays back wrong for wrong, but always try to be kind to each other and to everyone else."* If we think about the parallel with beavers creating a habitat, we can see that pastors and church planters could fall into this category of hard workers that the Lord has placed over us. The desire of the Holy Spirit is for Christians to operate in unity with one another as the body of Christ. We are to be kind to one another and help each other in our areas of weakness. As believers in Christ our mission is to create suitable habitats in the spirit and to build one another up in our faith. We should be creating some new ecosystems of grace and encouragement for other believers. Do you create a suitable habitat for others?

CAN YOU TAME YOUR TONGUE?

Have you ever had the experience of taming an animal? It could be as simple as training a puppy to do simple commands or habituating a reptile that you have caught in the wild to be accustomed to handling. As someone who works with animals on a regular basis I know that taming animals is all about consistency. You have to do the same things at the same times so that the animal gets used to you and understands that you don't mean it any harm. It can often be a frustrating process and even be cause for the occasional bite or scratch but the end result is far more rewarding.

James, the half brother of Jesus, talks about the taming of the tongue in the 3rd chapter of his epistle. James 3:7-8 says, *"All kinds of animals, birds, reptiles and sea creatures are being tamed and have been tamed by mankind, but no human being can tame the tongue. It is a restless evil, full of deadly poison."* This doesn't mean that we have free license to say anything we want but that in our own power we are incapable of taming our tongues. When we become believers in Christ we are made into a new creation and Jesus becomes Lord over our lives.

Jesus is able to tame even the vilest of tongues and use it for his glory. The unrepentant tongue can produce words that are like poison to the hearer. As believers we are called to bring life, not death. Scripture also says that we will be judged for every careless word we speak. We must remember that and be more cognizant of the words we speak. Let us speak life to those around us! Can you tame your tongue?

A HOGNOSE SNAKE PLAYS DEAD, DO YOU?

Have you ever had the opportunity to see a hognose snake? They have quite the display when they are threatened. When a hognose snake is startled it will hiss, spread its neck to appear larger and even venomous. They will sway back and forth like a cobra and mock strike at their aggressor. If all of that fails they simply play dead. They roll over on their back, stick out their tongue and produce the foulest of musk. They look dead, feel dead and even smell dead. For most predators this display will convince them not to eat the hognose and move on their way. Once the threat is gone the snake rights itself and crawls away.

How many times do we as Christians play dead in the sight of the predator of our souls, the devil? We know the commands of Christ to love one another and make disciples but we sit idly by and play dead in the pews or in our homes knowing that there needs to be action with our faith. James 1:22 says, *"Do not merely listen to the word, and so deceive yourselves. Do what it says."* James goes on to say in chapter 2:14 *"What good is it, my brothers, if a man claims to have faith but has no deeds? Can such faith save him?"*

Thankfully our salvation is a free gift and we don't have to earn it to be assured a place in heaven, but there are so many out there that are in desperate need of this saving faith that we have. Jesus wants us to have faith and to back our faith up with good deeds and truly living out his teaching and commands. If we just hear the word but do not do it are we living out this Christian life to the fullest or are we just playing dead? A hognose snake plays dead, do you?

CAN YOU DEFEND YOUR FAITH AGAINST A SASQUATCH?

I have been fascinated with the allure of Bigfoot (aka Sasquatch, Yeti, Skunk Ape, etc.) since I was a kid. I mean who hasn't watched that iconic Patterson film from the 1960's and wondered if it was in fact not a hoax but a potentially undiscovered large primate. I am the eternal skeptic though and often read stories about Bigfoot only to later see that they have been debunked as a fallacy or just someone's attempt at their 15 minutes of fame. I do, however, commend the Bigfoot community in their efforts to authenticate their findings and their tireless searching and research on the subject matter.

I wish I could say the same thing for the average Christian. Can you defend, or even explain your faith to an unbeliever? This is something Jude, the half-brother of Jesus felt very strongly about in the beginning of his epistle. Jude 1:3 says "*Dear friends, although I was very eager to write to you about the salvation we share, I felt I had to write and urge you to contend for the faith that was once for all entrusted to the saints.*"

Jude addresses fellow believers and it seems almost mid-thought he changes course from encouraging them about their shared salvation and begins pleading with them to contend for their faith. The mental imagery he was painting about defending the faith was something very physical, something reminiscent of a Roman gladiator fighting for his life. We are called to preach the word of God and proclaim His truth so we must know the word in order to defend it. I encourage you to pick up your sword of the spirit, which is the word of God, and start defending your faith. Can you defend your faith against a Sasquatch?

SPRING PEEPERS CARRY THEIR CROSS, DO YOU?

Every year around February I begin to get excited about the coming of spring. The first indicator for me that winter is loosing its grip is when I begin to hear winter breeding frogs like chorus frogs and spring peepers. The bird-like call of spring peepers gets me the most excited because conditions have to be warmer for them to come out than their cousins the chorus frogs. The spring peeper's Latin name is *Pseudacris crucifer*. They have a very prominent cross or X shape on their back, hence the species name "*crucifer.*"

They are a very visual representation of the crucifixion of Jesus and they even start their springtime reveling right before Easter. I tend to think of them as a proclamation of good news that winter is over and spring is about to begin. The death of winter is over and the new life of spring is just around the corner. Their timing with the celebration of the death, burial, and resurrection of Jesus Christ is icing on the cake.

We as believers in Jesus Christ need to be more like these frogs, visibly carrying our crosses but joyfully calling out and proclaiming the glory of God to a cold world. Matthew 16:24 says, *"Then Jesus said to his disciples, "If anyone would come after me, he must deny himself and take up his cross and follow me."* Even though spring peeper frogs are designed to withstand the cold of late winter and early spring, it still must be uncomfortable for them to emerge and dutifully announce the coming of spring. We as believers in Jesus Christ need to deny ourselves and pick up our crosses, so that a dying world can see that just around the corner spring has sprung. New life is on the way! Spring peepers carry their crosses, do you?

DO YOU SLEEP LIKE A BEAR?

Do you live in a place where bears can be frequently seen on spring and summer days? That must be terrifying! Lock your doors immediately! With all joking aside if you have ever noticed the behavior of bears you notice that their activity starts to slow down once the weather gets cold and pretty soon their sightings stop altogether for several months. During the cold winter month's bears will often hibernate because of a lack of available food. This process is quite interesting to me as their bodies simply slow down their metabolic processes and this allows them to essentially "sleep" through the harsher months.

How many times as Christians does it seem that when times get tough we will simply shut down and go to sleep? It is quite the easy route to take when we forget the power of Christ that resides in us. Our natural inclination is to just slow down our rate of activity in order to enter into false rest. When scripture talks of sleeping it usually is a metaphor for death, as in the case with Lazarus in the Gospel of John as well as in Ephesians.

Ephesians 5:13-14 says, *"But everything exposed by the light becomes visible, for it is light that makes everything visible. This is why it is said: 'Wake up, O sleeper, rise from the dead, and Christ will shine on you.'"* So even when times are hard and we just want to ball up and go to sleep both physically and spiritually we must remember that the light of Christ has illuminated us. Jesus calls us back to life and requires us to carry our cross even when it gets heavy. Do you sleep like a bear?

ARE YOU BEING LED BY A LEASH?

When I walk my dog I have to put him on a leash. It is not something I do to punish him but it's actually to protect him from himself and other outside forces like cars and people. If it were a perfect scenario, I would prefer him to walk beside me untethered and on occasion he is able to do so when there is sufficient room to roam and no urban hazards. The same is true with God's law.

God's law isn't here to punish us; in fact it's quite the opposite. God's law gives us an awareness of our sinfulness (Romans 7) as well as the standard to which we are to strive to live up to (Romans 3). God's law operates like the leash I put on my dog. Seeing that we are commanded not to murder, covet, etc. we know that these things are wrong and they give us parameters to live up to.

We can't use the law, however, to earn our salvation because our own righteousness is like filthy rags as said by the prophet Isaiah. We are to wear the righteousness of Christ because he is the fulfillment of the law. He is our righteousness and the freedom that we have and through his perfection. His sinlessness puts us in right standing with God as we accept him and humble ourselves to his lordship.

So just like when I use my authority to lead my dog by his leash I am doing so out of love for his wellbeing and safety because I see the dangers that he is oblivious to. The same is true for our heavenly Father. He sees throughout history the things that cause humanity to stumble into sin and He lovingly gives us His holy law for us to abide by so that we can avoid those pitfalls. The question is can you trust God to lovingly lead you, even if he pulls your "leash" and steers you somewhere you, in your shortsightedness, don't want to go? Are you being led by a leash?

DO YOU LIVE LIKE A SNAPPING TURTLE?

Snapping turtles (*Chelydra serpentina*) are large and aggressive turtles found in murky muddy water. They, like their surroundings, have somewhat of a dirty personality. They are quick to attack when threatened, hence the name, "snapping" turtle. These guys will feed on just about anything from plants to animals to carrion. If they can put it in their mouths they will eat it. They have a nasty disposition, live in nasty surroundings and eat nasty food. Does this seem like a theme with people you know? People can become a product of their environment and only feed their spirit with garbage and murk and what goes in must come out.

Snapping turtles spend so much time in the mud that they even look like mud; they in many ways have conformed to the world around them and are as dirty as the mud holes they live in. It says in Romans 12:2 *"Do not conform any longer to the pattern of this world, but be transformed by the renewing of your mind. Then you will be able to test and approve what God's will is—his good, pleasing and perfect will."*

HAVE YOU BEEN SET FREE LIKE A WILD HORSE?

Have you ever seen a truly wild horse? Recently I was privileged enough to see a group of wild horses in the Outer Banks of NC and it struck me that their freedom is what sets them apart from captive horses. Jesus came to liberate us from sin and death and a life with him is one that is truly free. Captive horses live within small parameters and are often oblivious to what a life of true freedom even looks like. Galatians 5:1 says "*It is for freedom that Christ has set us free. Stand firm, then, and do not let yourselves be burdened again by a yoke of slavery.*"

When the Spanish ran aground in the 16th and 17th centuries along the North Carolina coast the first thing to go were the heavy horses that they carried from Spain. How often is our freedom in Christ the first thing to go when we are ran aground by life's circumstances? The horses went from a life of captive slavery to one of complete freedom in a matter of moments as they scrambled to swim to the shore. It seems representative of our walk with Christ in that sometimes it takes a push of tragedy or even just a moment of helplessness to regain our freedom in Christ and remember that He has set us free.

JELLYFISH DON'T HAVE BACKBONES, DO YOU?

Have you ever really looked at the nature and body type of a jellyfish? They are considered invertebrates, which simply means they have no backbone. How many times do we as believers operate more like invertebrates with no backbone in the face of spiritual adversity? Jesus is calling us to stand up for him and loudly proclaim our faith, not just the things that are comfortable and easy to digest. Matthew 11:12 says *"From the days of John the Baptist until now, the kingdom of heaven has been forcefully advancing, and forceful men lay hold of it."*

If you have seen a jellyfish in it's own environment it moves effortlessly and if approached it will sting you with its tentacles. Once it washes up on shore, out of it's comfort zone, it no longer has much of a defense and will ultimately die in the sun. They just don't have the ability to stand up and walk back into the sea; their tentacles are good for quick defense but useless for moving on land. Jesus is calling us to be less like jellyfish and more like men such as John the Baptist. We need to be willing to take the Kingdom of Heaven by force and stand up for Christ both in and out of our element. Christ made us vertebrates (with backbones) in His image - let's start acting like it!

ARE YOU A GOOD MIMIC?

What does it mean to be a mimic? In the case of some animals like the Scarlet King snake it is a benefit biologically because other animals will regard them as something else and will not take a chance on eating them for fear of being injured or killed themselves. So looking or acting like something else is beneficial to that organism because of the association to the thing they are mimicking. Couldn't that also work with Christians as well?

The term "Christian" defined by one online dictionary is as follows: "Manifesting the qualities or spirit of Jesus; Christ like." Ephesians 5:1-2 in the NIV says *"Follow God's example, therefore, as dearly loved children and walk in the way of love, just as Christ loved us and gave himself up for us as a fragrant offering and sacrifice to God."* The New King James Version has it translated as *"Therefore be imitators of God as dear children. And walk in love, as Christ also has loved us and given Himself for us, an offering and a sacrifice to God for a sweet-smelling aroma."* So if we look at being a mimic, or imitator, in the context of those scriptures and apply that to why animals are found as mimics in nature what can we gather? How can we mimic Christ more effectively?

One way we can mimic Jesus is to look at how we are supposed to treat others in light of Matthew 5:38-48. *"You have heard that it was said, 'Eye for eye, and tooth for tooth.' But I tell you, do not resist an evil person. If anyone slaps you on the right cheek, turn to them the other cheek also. And if anyone wants to sue you and take your shirt, hand over your coat as well. If anyone forces you to go one mile, go with them two miles. Give to the one who asks you, and do not turn away from the one who wants to borrow from you. "You have heard that it was said, 'Love your neighbor and hate your enemy.' But I tell you, love your enemies and pray for those who persecute you, that you may be children of your Father in heaven. He causes his sun to rise on the evil and the good, and sends rain on the righteous and the unrighteous. If you love those who love you, what reward will you get? Are not even the tax collectors doing that? And if you greet only your own people, what are you doing more than others? Do not even pagans do that? Be perfect, therefore, as your heavenly Father is perfect."*

Jesus says we have to turn the other cheek and essentially not let the world get to us, mimic Jesus in peace and humility and not go around looking for a fight or a chance to prove ourselves to everyone in violence or other areas of our lives. We have to go the extra mile with people and not expect immediate results as well as give them more than they even asked for in the first place. In order to effectively mimic Jesus we must actually love our neighbors AND our enemies. That's kind of a tough pill to swallow. I thought that we could mimic Jesus by wearing WWJD bracelets and crucifix necklaces all the time. Surely that will work right? It's easy to love those that love us, it's even easier to always live in our Christian bubbles and never get out into the world and actually love those that may curse us for doing so. Jesus ends this verse with a call to mimic him by saying *"Be perfect, therefore, as your heavenly Father is perfect."* Will you drop the charade and start loving people in the name of Jesus? Lets be imitators of Christ and mimic the Father so our enemies will not see us as who we are but as who He is.

SPARROWS DON'T WORRY, DO YOU?

The other day as I was sitting outside on the patio of a local Starbucks reading, I kept noticing the cute little sparrows chirping and hopping around. My eyes were immediately transfixed on one little male that was joyfully scarfing down some breadcrumbs that had fallen between the cracks on the bricks. As my eyes were locked on his mid afternoon meal consumption, the thought hit me. What if our faith in God and His provision is just like following breadcrumbs. I know for me personally it seems that outside of the Lord providing the next crumb we wouldn't even have breadcrumbs to eat. I am constantly battling with my lack of faith in the provision of our heavenly Father but as this little sparrow reminded me, faith sometimes just looks like chasing breadcrumbs and believing there will be more crumbs tomorrow.

Jesus says in Matthew 6:25-27 *"Therefore I tell you, do not worry about your life, what you will eat or drink; or about your body, what you will wear. Is not life more than food, and the body more than clothes? Look at the birds of the air; they do not sow or reap or store away in barns, and yet your heavenly Father feeds them. Are you not much more valuable than they? Can any one of you by worrying add a single hour to your life?"* When I find myself worrying about provision I have to remind myself that the birds are provided for daily and they sing God's praises all day long. They seem to know something that I have yet to grasp, that is our Father really does love us and has our best interest at heart and WILL take care of us.

Jesus affirms that again in Matthew 10:29-31 *"Are not two sparrows sold for a penny? Yet not one of them will fall to the ground outside your Father's care. And even the very hairs of your head are all numbered. So don't be afraid; you are worth more than many sparrows."* Jesus knows what you are struggling with and what your needs are, He even knows how many hairs are on your head. He loves you enough to know all the specifics so next time you start to worry, remember that he will take care of the sparrows but loves and cares for you even more.

HOMING PIGEONS CAN GET BACK HOME, CAN YOU?

Have you ever heard of a bird called a homing pigeon? They are a type of pigeon descended from a rock pigeon that has an innate ability to find its way home. Some have been observed coming home after flying hundreds if not thousands of miles. The same is true for Christians that may lose their way. A homing pigeon is similar to the prodigal son in that once it has gone far away from home, it realizes it needs to return to the place that it's from.

Luke 15:24 says *"For this son of mine was dead and is alive again; he was lost and is found.' So they began to celebrate."* Before we found and accepted Jesus we were all dead in our sins. Some of us even after we accept Jesus find ourselves far from home just as the prodigal son found himself. The sooner we come back to our senses and find our way back home to Jesus the better.

He is there ready and waiting to forgive us with open arms just as the father in the story of the prodigal son. Just like the homing pigeon knows exactly how to get home, we as believers know exactly how to get back to Jesus and that's humbly through our prayers and petitions for forgiveness. Homing pigeons can get back home, can you?

ARE YOU THE VENOM OR THE CURE?

One of the groups of animals I am most fascinated with are pit vipers and other venomous snakes. They are perceived as something inherently evil and of no value to humankind but that couldn't be further from the truth. I genuinely believe that if God created it then it's good and sometimes we just have to dig and find its goodness. In the case of pit vipers and other not so favorable venomous snakes there is the potential for benefit to humans through the very thing people are afraid of, the venom. Did you know that scientists are using snake venom to help find cures and treatments to things such as cancer, strokes, heart problems and many other diseases? Venom is all a matter of context. To those on the receiving end of an angry bite venom produces death, but to those in the operating room being treated with a serum derived of snake venom, it brings life.

The same thing is true with the words we speak as Christians to an unbelieving world. Proverbs 18:21 says, *"The tongue has the power of life and death, and those who love it will eat its fruit."* I don't think it's a coincidence that this verse references the tongue and eating fruit. If we rewind scripture a few chapters back we are reminded of an event that took place in Genesis chapter 3 where a snake deceived Adam and Eve and they ate from the tree of knowledge of good and evil. Once they tasted of that tree they were no longer allowed to eat from the tree of life.

When we use our tongue to bash fellow Christians or say things to offend those in the world, then we are not eating from the tree of life. We are speaking death and even though the words we may be saying may have the essence of life to them, the context in which they are received relegates them to death. We must choose our words carefully and truly try to speak the truths of God in love so that they are received in the proper context. Are you the venom or the cure?

DO YOU HAVE FAITH LIKE A FROG?

Did you know that some frogs take care of their babies? The Blue Jeans Dart Frog, *Oophaga pumilio*, (formerly *Dendrobates pumilio*) actually carries its babies on its back to deposit them in suitable habitats, like the funnels of bromeliad plants. They do this because, as a loving parent should, they care how their children will grow up.

Do you know that our heavenly Father does the same thing? He cares how we will grow up and helps to place us in the right habitat so that we will be able to grow up and do His will. Do you have faith like a frog? Do you believe that the Father has got you taken care of? 1 Peter 5:7 says *"Cast all your anxiety on him because he cares for you."*

Just like in the case of baby blue jeans frogs, we must rely on the knowledge of the father, have faith that He has our best interest at heart, and hold on for the ride. If this little frog cares for its children, think about how much more our heavenly Father cares about us. So I will ask you again, do you have faith like a frog? (Also read Matthew 6:25-34)

ARE YOU CALM IN THE STORM?

Have you ever noticed that storms are exciting when you know they are coming, but if one catches you off guard it is an almost entirely different experience? I remember thinking this one day as I walked in the woods and saw storm clouds coming. I knew this one was approaching and wanted to watch it. I was anxiously awaiting the claps of thunder and flashes of lightening. It was exciting to me to see the cumulonimbus clouds get bigger and blacker. I was prepared for this storm and because of that it seemed different than if I were caught off guard.

The exact opposite experience took place on the ocean one day when we were unwittingly under a small craft advisory and the 6-8 foot swells were swamping our extremely small boat. I remember thinking I was going to die and trying to ascertain the best way to jump if the boat began to capsize. "Okay, if the bubbles go up I swim that way to the surface," these were things that flashed through my mind during this unexpected storm. Almost in a moment, Jesus made himself known to me as I was praying silently on the bow of the boat and reminded me to focus on him.

How many times do we let the storms of life take control when Jesus has full power and authority to calm the wind and waves in our lives? Although the waves didn't get any smaller and our boat didn't feel any more seaworthy, I felt peace. Once my focus shifted from the storm and my situation back to Jesus my whole outlook changed. I was prepared once again to enjoy the storm and be excited for the adventure because Jesus was in full control. This experience really made *Mark 4:35-41* come alive to me. Our focus needs to constantly be on Jesus. Are you calm in the storm?

JOSHUA 9:10–10:6
country. We came because
great power of the LORD
heard about what he has
everything he did in
heard that he defeated
Amorites east of the Jordan
King Sihon of Heshbon
Bashan in the land
elders* and our people
enough food for your
with the Israelites
your servants
with us.'
14"Look at
home, it was
can see the
wineskins
JOSHUA 10:7–30
ountry was brave enough to
ast the Israelites.
Move the rocks
ance to the cave.
23So Joshua's men
s out of the cave—the
Hebron, Jarmuth,
When they brought
he called all his
kings. He said to the
came close
afraid.
Land for Benjamin
of Benjamin was given
between the areas of Judah
family in the tribe of
This is the land that
Benjamin: 12The north
the Jordan River. It went
edge of Jericho.
went into the hill country
was just east of
the border went south to
Beth Horon.
lites, "Why do
your land? The
fathers, has given
each of your tribes
men. I will send them
and. They will describe
they will come back to
divide the land into seven
ple of Judah will keep their
outh. The people of Joseph will
land in the north. 6But you
escribe the land and divide it into
parts. Bring the map to me, and we
the LORD our God decide which
will get which land.a 7The Levites
get a share of the land. Their share is
to serve the LORD as priests. God, Reuben,
and half the tribe of Manasseh have already
received the land that was promised
them. They are on the east side of the
Jordan River. Moses, the LORD's servant,
gave them that land."
8So the men who were chosen went to
look at the land and write down what they
saw. Joshua told them, "Go through the
land and describe it in writing. Then come
back to me at Shiloh. I will throw lots* and
the LORD divide the land for you."
men went into the land. As they
walked through it, they wrote down what
they saw. They listed all the cities and
divided the land into seven parts. Then
they went back to Joshua at Shiloh.
a18:6 we ... land Literally, "I will throw lots here before the LORD our God."
hal), then down to Ataroth Addar
Beth Horon.
Horon, the border turned south and
along the west side of the hill. The
went to Kiriath Baal (also called
Jearim), this town belonged to the
of Judah. This was the western border.
15The southern border started
Kiriath Jearim and went to the
Nephtoah. 16Then the border
to the bottom of the hill near the
Ben Hinnom, north of Rephaim
continued down Hinnom Valley
of the Jebusite city. Then the border
on to Rogel. There it turned
went to En Shemesh, and then continued
on to Geliloth. (Geliloth is near the
mim Pass in the mountains.) The
went down to the Great Stone that
named for Bohan, the son of Reuben.
continued to the northern part of
Arabah. Then the border went down
the Jordan Valley. 19Then it went
northern part of Beth Hoglah and ended
the north shore of the Dead Sea.
where the Jordan River flows into
That was the southern border.
20The Jordan River was the east
border. So this was the land that was
to the tribe of Benjamin. These were
borders on all sides. 21Each family
land. These are their cities: Jericho,
Hoglah, Emek Keziz, 22Beth
Zemaraim, Bethel, 23Avvim, Parah,
24Kephar Ammoni, Ophni, and
There were twelve cities and the
around them.
25The tribe of Benjamin also got
Ramah, Beeroth, 26Mizpah,
Mozah, 27Rekem, Irpeel, Taralah,
Haeleph, the Jebusite city
Jerusalem), Gibeah, and Kiriath
Land for

ARE YOU DEVOTED TO DESTRUCTION?

This morning while I was reading Joshua 7 something leapt off the page and started to really make me think. Joshua 7:12 in the second half of the verse says *"...I will not be with you anymore unless you destroy whatever among you is devoted to destruction."* I realize through previous scriptures in Deuteronomy and again repeated in the New Testament that the Lord will never leave me nor forsake me but this verse posed an interesting thought. Do my actions really have consequences?

The context of the verse involves the people of Israel coming out of the wilderness and claiming the Promised Land the Lord has given to them. They have obeyed the commands and instructions of God and had victory in the land up to this point. They go into battle and something goes wrong, they are forced to retreat and around 36 men are killed. This is the result of one man's disobedience. Achor disobeyed God by keeping some of the plunder of the land for himself and hiding it in his tent. This caused the favor of God to leave the Israelites in battle and forced their retreat as well as the casualties.

How many times do we disobey God and create our own destruction by doing our own thing? The sin of Achor affected his whole family as well as his community. 36 men died and he and his family were stoned and burned because of his disobedience. This is obviously an extreme case but it makes the point that although we have grace thankfully now because of God sending His one and only son, Jesus Christ, into the world; we still need to be aware of our sins and disobedience because they have consequences. We need to rid ourselves of the sins in our lives that lead to destruction. Lord I pray we humble ourselves and admit when we are wrong, and that by the blood of Jesus you forgive us of the many sins we commit against you. Are you devoted to destruction?

DO YOU GRUMBLE IN THE WILDERNESS?

Have you ever been lost in the woods before? I mean really lost. I have to say that I have been lost in the wilderness more times than I would like to admit, especially since I spend most of my waking hours in or near the woods. One time that is specifically seared into my brain happened on a family outing when I was in elementary school. My family and I somehow got off the well-marked trail at a well known hiking place near my home and as the sun started to set we stumbled further and further away from the orange blazes that marked our trail. I distinctly remember vocalizing my complaints, my fears, and my dread that we may die in the woods on this autumn night. I had a good deal of fear and frustration running through my brain and lips. What if we never made it home? We became grumpier and grumpier the longer we were lost, until my brother leaned up against a sign signaling the direction to the parking lot.

Moses seemed to have a similar situation with the people of Israel when the Lord liberated them from the nation of Egypt. Exodus 16:1-3 says. *"The whole Israelite community set out from Elim and came to the Desert of Sin, which is between Elim and Sinai, on the fifteenth day of the second month after they had come out of Egypt. In the desert the whole community grumbled against Moses and Aaron. The Israelites said to them, "If only we had died by the LORD's hand in Egypt! There we sat around pots of meat and ate all the food we wanted, but you have brought us out into this desert to starve this entire assembly to death."* The Lord showed the people of Israel patience time and time again by sparing them despite their grumbling and complaining, but not without punishment. Had the people been obedient to the man of God placed before them and had faith, their 40 year journey could have been completed in less than a year and they could have enjoyed the promise land much sooner.

How many times do we grumble against God when we should really be praising Him for the provision we do have? With our limited vision our situation always seems much worse than it is and we could literally be leaning against the sign that signals our deliverance, if only we would stop grumbling long enough to look. Do you grumble in the wilderness?

TRAIL

ARE YOU FULL OF BUGS?

Recently while walking near a trail in the woods I kicked open a rotting pine log to see if anyone was living inside. Much to my chagrin I found tons of termites, it was absolutely teeming with the little guys! In that moment I had the thought that just as this tree had to die for these termites to have life we too must die to ourselves so that Christ can be fully alive inside of us. Galatians 2:20 says "*I have been crucified with Christ and I no longer live, but Christ lives in me. The life I now live in the body, I live by faith in the Son of God, who loved me and gave himself for me.*"

A tree has to either be sick or dead for termites to really infest it like this and it makes sense even in the spiritual because we must first be aware that we are sick with our own sin and then die to it before Christ can truly infest our core. Just like the termites made a dead tree teem with life on the inside, Christ can make a dead human alive with his redemptive grace. Are you willing to lay down your life so that Christ can live in you? Are you full of Bugs?

ARE YOU LASHING OUT LIKE A CORNERED ANIMAL?

One of my favorite activities is to study an animal and its ecosystem and try to locate and eventually capture said animal. Often I will back an animal, like a snake, into a corner and if I don't act quickly while trying to capture it, I can find myself on the receiving end of angry teeth. Biologically animals (and humans) are designed with a mechanism that enables them to react with either fight or flight.

When animals are put into a stressful situation that fight or flight mechanism takes over and they either flee or stay and address the aggressor. I find myself being stressed out all too often and reacting out of a fight or flight mindset more than I would like to admit. Psalm 55:22 says "*Cast your cares on the Lord and he will sustain you; he will never let the righteous be shaken.*" Next time you feel that surging of adrenaline that signifies the oncoming reaction to stress and you feel like fighting or fleeing from the situation remember that Jesus overcame the world and as you accept Him you take on His righteousness (Romans 3:22). So tell God about your problem and He won't let you be shaken. Are you lashing out like a cornered animal?

CAN YOU ADAPT WHEN TIMES GET TOUGH?

With the onset of the gloom and cold of winter I often find myself marveling at the adaptations some animals go through just to survive the tough times of the season. Amphibians are exothermic, or cold blooded, and that means that when the temperatures drop so does their metabolism and activity. If a frog is so tempted to stay above ground during this time of year it often signifies their certain demise. There is one species of frog that seems to be the exception to this rule. The Wood Frog, *Rana sylvatica*, has the ability to completely freeze and once temperatures are optimal again it can essentially thaw out and resume life as normal. This is due to the production of glucose in the frog's body that acts as biological antifreeze.

We can make a scriptural parallel when we think about how our God has given us the tools we need to survive the harshest of times. This idea appears in Ephesians 6:10-20 with the full armor of God as well as in other verses like 1 Corinthians 10:13. If we look at the latter verse, 1 Corinthians 10:13, we see that God will not allow temptation to overtake us without a way of escape. In the case of the frog the harshness of winter's chill will not kill the frog because it can endure the frigid temperatures, because God designed it with a biological way out. Like the frog's way of escape, when we are faced with temptations, God has given us a spiritual way out through prayer and the reading of His word. Can you adapt when times get tough like the Wood Frog?

ARE YOU LIVING ON AN ANTIQUATED FAITH?

Aside from animals, I have a growing passion for antique books. I don't really ever do much more than flip through them, but I'm somewhat of a book nerd. I love the way they look, smell and feel. I just love old books! I really like old religion or science books as you can probably imagine. My wife and I stopped at an old used bookstore somewhere in Virginia on our way to visit friends in Virginia Beach a few years ago.

Amid the acrid smelling volumes of books seemingly strewn any which way, we discovered a small biology textbook from the 1930's. I was even more excited to see that the price tag on the book was somewhere in the $2 range. Definitely in my budget! So as we were walking through the historic district of this small town I decided to flip through my "Dynamic Biology" textbook from almost 100 years ago and marveled at the beautifully drawn sketches and worn pages. When we got home I put it on display on my bookshelf and didn't think much of it until a few weeks later.

I began to think about how if we don't update our faith, if we don't live from glory to glory as it says in 2 Corinthians 3:18 then we are only reflecting antiquated information to the world. See the information in the old textbook I found is great but it's not current. If you were to look in the back of the book you will notice a glaring deficiency somewhere in the D section of its glossary. There is no mention of DNA. This volume of "Dynamic Biology" predates the discovery of the double helix structure by Watson and Crick and is thus antiquated for effective use. How often are we merely living in the past and not updating our faith? Are you living on an antiquated faith?

BUMPER BOOK
BLACK BEAUTY
THE GOOD HANDYMAN'S ENCYCLOPEDIA
TALES OF WELLS FARGO
ARTHUR MEE'S WONDERFUL DAY
IN THE SERVICE OF THE PEACOCK THRONE
TALES OF TEXAS RANGERS
Jack and Jill BOOK
ANNUAL
ANNUAL 1973
PLAYWAYS ANNUAL
MODERN MARVELS OF SCIENCE
A GIANT PICTURE DICTIONARY
TAMMY ANNUAL 1974
FOOTBALL
BOTANIC MAN
DAVID BELLAMY

ARE YOU PREPARED FOR A NOCTURNAL THIEF?

Ever since I was a kid I have had a strange fascination with raccoons. These masked bandits in the night are one of my favorite animals. I love their mischievous behavior and sneaky antics and most of all their intelligence. If you've ever been camping someplace wilder than a suburban backyard you know that if food is left out in your camp you may be awakened by devious nocturnal thieves. Raccoons love to invade a campsite and ravage anything left out if things aren't properly stored.

When I think of scriptures that parallel an animal or the activities of an animal it's not a far stretch to think about the nature of raccoons and 1 Thessalonians 5:1-6. This scripture says *Now, brothers and sisters, about times and dates we do not need to write to you, for you know very well that the day of the Lord will come like a thief in the night. While people are saying, "Peace and safety," destruction will come on them suddenly, as labor pains on a pregnant woman, and they will not escape. But you, brothers and sisters, are not in darkness so that this day should surprise you like a thief. You are all children of the light and children of the day. We do not belong to the night or to the darkness. So then, let us not be like others, who are asleep, but let us be awake and sober.*

As believers in Jesus Christ we shouldn't worry about when the end will come nor shall we worry about the false security preached by so many false prophets of the day. We just need to be adequately prepared by accepting Jesus Christ as our Savior and living true to His word. We know our security is in our Lord Jesus Christ and if we continue to live in the light of day we will not be surprised by a thief in the night. We are not nocturnal creatures like my favorite animal buddy, the raccoon, happens to be. So the things we do are done in the light in full view of the world. Are you prepared for a nocturnal thief?

DO YOU LOVE YOUR BROTHER LIKE A GOLDEN EAGLE?

When I was a kid I got a rather large book on eagles and other birds of prey from my grandmother one year for Christmas. I studied that book, drew pictures of the different birds, and daydreamed about one day seeing them in the wild. I was pretty shocked to learn that when a golden eagle (and numerous other eagle species) lay more than one egg in a nest, often the first one to hatch will kill the weaker second born. In terms of survival this is advantageous to the firstborn eaglet but horrific for the second. Although this deals with real aspects of life and death, how often do we do the exact same thing to our brothers and sisters in Christ?

Isn't it easy to steal spiritual food from our Christian brothers and sisters in hopes of selfishly growing faster than those around us? We can unknowingly be causing fratricide in the body of Christ by not appropriately loving those around us that God has placed in the family of believers. 1 John 4:20 says, *"Whoever claims to love God yet hates a brother or sister is a liar. For whoever does not love their brother and sister, whom they have seen, cannot love God, whom they have not seen."* In our pursuit of holiness we can often leave in our wake any number of people that we have held unforgiveness for or simply not given an adequate amount of genuine love. Christ, through the Apostle John, challenges us to truly love one another so that we can really love God. Do you love your brother like a golden eagle?

ARE YOU THE HONEY OR THE STING?

What's the first thing that pops into your head when you think of bees? I'm betting that beestings and angry swarms popped in your head, and then in a distant third place you may think of honey. Ok so what's the first thing you think of when you hear the word "Christian?" If I were to ask someone outside of church culture that question I'm betting some adjectives would include judgmental, narrow minded, and then maybe in a distant third place people may say something about love, maybe. All to often people relate Christians to the sting created by our lack of love in practice. If honey is the "fruit" produced by a beehive that is functioning normally then love should be the fruit produced by a church functioning normally.

Honey has been used as an antiseptic, an energy booster, a preservative and a tasty treat among other things. Just like the sweetness of honey, the work of Jesus on the Cross and the love Christ endured to take on that task is as sweet as honey. The love of Christ is the job of the Church to reflect into the world. John 13:34-35 says *"A new command I give you: Love one another. As I have loved you, so you must love one another. 35 By this all men will know that you are my disciples, if you love one another."* Jesus isn't suggesting or even politely asking us to love one another, he commands it. So just as a beehive works in perfect unity, harmony and perhaps even love to produce honey, we as the church should do the same and love one another so that the world is drawn to our sweetness and not scared away by our sting. Are you the honey or the sting?

ARE YOU WANDERING AROUND LIKE A MANGY MUTT?

Today I got the opportunity to visit my grandmother in my hometown of Trinity, North Carolina. After my visit was over I dropped off some mail in the small post office in town and as I was about to get out of my car to enter the tiny building something shaggy and reddish brown caught my eye. I looked for a second and what appeared to be Chewbacca's 2nd cousin was creeping towards me. It was a mangy matted and dreadlocked stray dog. I kept my eye on him trying to gauge whether he would be a friendly dog or some rabid beast that I should prepare to defend myself against.

I went into the post office and dropped off the letters I brought and when I came back to the parking lot the dog was still there. As I got closer to the dog and knelt down I reached my hand out, prepared myself for a diseased bite but instead found myself petting an incredibly sweet and shy dog that just seemed to have lost its way. I genuinely felt sad for this abandoned animal and I wish I could say that this story ended with me taking him home and rescuing him from the cold but I'm afraid my apartment zoo is at max capacity for animal life.

I stayed and nurtured the poor miserable dog for a few minutes and as I drove away I prayed that someone would come along and save the poor dog. As I was driving I was reminded of Romans 7:24 where Paul says *"What a wretched man I am! Who will rescue me from this body of death?"* This related perfectly to this stray dog. On first appearances this animal simply looked wretched to put it in a word and if no one shows up to redeem him, sadly, I fear this animal may end up dying.

This relates to us in that before we accepted Christ we were looked on by God as wretched human beings, stray and malnourished wandering helplessly on earth with no hope for redemption but the good news is that Christ died for just that reason and He has offered us redemption in the form of His sacrifice on the cross. Has Jesus Christ rescued you from your hapless wandering as a stray? Are you wandering around like a mangy mutt?

DO YOU SING LIKE A BIRD?

Birds truly inspire me to worship God and focus on proclaiming how awesome He is. Birds sing all day long, I've even heard them sing in the rain! They are such a great example of how we are to live as believers and followers of Jesus Christ. Psalm 145:21 says, *"My mouth will speak in praise to the LORD. Let every creature praise his holy name for ever and ever."*

The Psalmist proclaims that his mouth will speak in praise to the Lord. Every time I hear birds singing I think about them singing praises to our God. Psalm 96:11-13 says *"Let the heavens rejoice, let the earth be glad; let the sea resound, and all that is in it. Let the fields be jubilant, and everything in them; let all the trees of the forest sing for joy. Let all creation rejoice before the LORD, for he comes, he comes to judge the earth. He will judge the world in righteousness and the peoples in his faithfulness."* Since our God is the Creator of all things, it is only fitting that His creation worships Him in thankfulness. Have you ever thought about birds singing praises to God or the trees joyfully singing in worship to their creator? Do you sing like a bird?

ARE YOU BLIND LIKE A BAT?

Although a bat has pretty good eyesight, contrary to popular belief, they do not rely on their eyes to capture their prey. A bat operates in a nocturnal world and uses a process called echolocation to track down their in flight meals. Echolocation is essentially mammalian sonar and is basically a signal sent out and returned that helps them hone in on their objective. 2 Corinthians 5:7 says *"For we live by faith, not by sight."*

Did you know a bat could eat close to its body weight in mosquitoes every night? They literally eat thousands of these pesky bloodsuckers every night! As Christ followers we live by faith and not by sight just like it says in 2 Corinthians 5:7. So when you think of how a bat finds its way in the dark think about how we pray and send signals to God. The more we pray the easier it is to find our way.

Are you operating in faith? How is the signal that you're sending out? Maybe we can take a lesson from the bats and exercise our faith by sending some vocalizations to the Father in heaven to help us hone in on the will of God through prayer. Are you blind like a bat?

ARE YOU WATERING GRASS THAT'S JUST GOING TO WITHER?

Have you ever thought about how much time you spend on trivial things like making sure the lawn is perfectly manicured or the flower garden is adequately planted with the prettiest blooms? Isn't it easy to get carried away in the pursuit of perfection or attainment of "yard of the month" and neglect the things that truly need our attention? 1 Peter 1:24-25 says *"For, 'All men are like grass, and all their glory is like the flowers of the field; the grass withers and the flowers fall, but the word of the Lord stands forever.' And this is the word that was preached to you."*

This scripture is comparing our lives to withering grass and falling flowers. The good news is that God's word stands the test of time and we can rest assured that the time we spend studying the word of God is time well spent. The word that is preached to us, the Gospel of Jesus Christ, is timeless, everlasting and has the utmost importance and staying power. Our mortality is just as real as that of a flower fading and grass withering in the context of eternity. When we root ourselves in God's word we will not wither and we will not fade because the result is an eternity with Jesus where there is no more death. That's an amazing thought! Are you watering grass that's just going to wither?

ARE YOU PUTTING YOUR HEAD IN THE SAND?

There is a common misconception that ostriches hide their heads in the sand when threatened. This is simply a myth and it can be traced back as far as Pliny the Elder from the 1st century AD, around the same time that Jesus was on the Earth. In keeping with the mental image though, how many times does it appear that the Church seems to be merely putting her head in the sand and not truly engaging the threats or issues that arise? Do you feel that it's easier to hide out in the Church rather than engaging culture in Jesus name? As a group of Christians are we known more for our love and compassion for our fellow man or are we possibly viewed in the same light as the ostrich with his head in the sand? How can we change that perception?

Since we as believers in Jesus are the physical representation on the Earth of our heavenly Father we could perhaps start following his teachings. In a true reflection of the glory of Christ we could begin with loving our neighbor as ourselves or treating others with love and compassion and gracefully sharing our faith. John 13:35 says *"By this all men will know that you are my disciples, if you love one another."* We have to begin by loving one another in the body of Christ and from that love and unity share our love with the world. We've got some work to do but I believe in Jesus name we can accomplish it together. Are you putting your head in the sand?

DO YOU LIVE LIKE A FERAL CAT?

Have you ever driven behind a restaurant only to see massive quantities of feline scavengers? When a cat looses its desire to be captive and domesticated it will revert to a wild, or feral state. In many cases they retain some semblance of their former life in the first generation, but their offspring are often so wild they are untamable. This can lead to all sorts of trouble for both cats and people. Feral cats are a destructive, disease carrying menace that often preys on native wildlife and destroys the ecology of native species.

The people of Israel began to act as if they were feral in the land promised to their forefathers after Joshua and the elders of his generation died out. They were the second generation so to speak and began to take on the wild tendencies of a feral animal. Judges 2:10-14 says, "*After that whole generation had been gathered to their fathers, another generation grew up, who knew neither the LORD* nor what he had done for Israel. *[11] Then the Israelites did evil in the eyes of the LORD* and served the Baals. *[12] They forsook the LORD,* the God of their fathers, who had brought them out of Egypt. They followed and worshiped various gods of the peoples around them. They provoked the *LORD* to anger *[13] because they forsook him and served Baal and the Ashtoreths. [14] In his anger against Israel the LORD* handed them over to raiders who plundered them. He sold them to their enemies all around, whom they were no longer able to resist."

The fate of feral cats often includes capture and detainment in shelters, euthanasia, disease, and harmful interactions with traffic. If they would stay close to the hand that feeds them they would enjoy the safety and provision of a loving home, but when they decide to go wild and do things their own way the outcome is much more destructive to them. The same is true of the people of God. When we are in relationship with the Lord we can enjoy the comforts of our loving Father, but if we are not in covenant as believers with Jesus then we can only expect destruction. Do you live like a feral cat?

ARE YOU STUCK IN A CAVE?

Call me weird but I have always been excited about the mystery of caves, mines and other large holes in the Earth. There is just a certain level of the unknown that draws me in to explore every time. You just never know what to expect in that sort of environment. There is danger and intrigue at every turn and so long as you have faith in the life of your flashlight batteries, things will go well. Even though you can't see without your headlamp in most cases you rely on the equipment and preparation to get you to the surface.

Hebrews 11:1-2 says, *"Now faith is being sure of what we hope for and certain of what we do not see. This is what the ancients were commended for."* When we walk with Jesus sometimes it feels as if we are truly walking in a dark tunnel or cave. We know He has led us and He will not leave nor forsake us, but sometimes it just feels dark. Thankfully in these moments we can rely on the faith that we have to get us through. We are sure of the hope we have in Christ because we believe that Jesus won't just leave us in the dark. Sometimes we just need to take that step of faith and truly trust and believe Jesus even if it feels like we are in the depths of a dark cave. Jesus requires our devotion and our trust and He will see us to the other side of eternity. I can put faith in Him for that. Are you stuck in a cave?

ARE YOU PATIENT LIKE AN ALLIGATOR?

Have you ever watched an alligator move ever so slowly while stalking its prey? They seem to have a large measure of patience while gradually inching closer and closer to their target. Some will even lay on the bottom of the swamp with their mouth open and patiently wait for an easy meal like a fish to swim into their toothy trap. Then just at the right time - SNAP! Their jaws will lock down on the meal they have been waiting all day for. The end result of their wait is the reward they were hoping for, a meal.

Romans 8:24-25 says, *"For in this hope we were saved. Now hope that is seen is not hope. For who hopes for what he sees? But if we hope for what we do not see, we wait for it with patience."* As believers we are waiting patiently in expectation of the return of Jesus. We believe He is who He says He is and live our lives accordingly. The reward for our faith and patience is an eternity in Heaven with our Creator. Just like the alligator waits in anticipation of his next meal, we as believers wait in expectation for the Lord. Are you patient like an alligator?

WHAT'S YOUR EXCUSE?

I often wonder why it took me so long to come to faith in Jesus Christ when His creation speaks so loudly of His existence. If you have ever walked through the woods alone and were awestruck by the beauty therein or if you have ever seen a breathtaking sunset or ocean view, you must at least realize that these things didn't happen by chance.

Romans 1 says "*For since the creation of the world God's invisible qualities--his eternal power and divine nature--have been clearly seen, being understood from what has been made, so that men are without excuse.*" Often it seems we can find any and every excuse to discount God's handiwork, even in our own lives, but the truth is that God is the Creator of our universe and even our own lives. When we take the time to swallow our pride and give credit where credit is due we can humbly see that God does truly love us, even simply by just the things around us He created just for us to enjoy. Next time you are out in creation or even just stuck in traffic, give God thanks for all that He has made and be thankful you were on the list of His created things! What's your excuse?

HOOK ARTIFICIAL LURES ONLY
Wildlife
INCHES DAILY
MAY KEEP ONLY

CONCLUSION

Have you ever thought of Jesus as a gardener? Mary Magdalene, upon finding the empty tomb in John 20, saw a man who she supposed was a gardener until he called her by name. She was distressed and upset that this man, the gardener, didn't realize they had taken her Lord away. As soon as the "gardener" says "Mary" she knows it's her Lord Jesus, and He has risen from the grave!

I don't think her confusion was a coincidence. I think Jesus made a statement and was intentional in appearing as a gardener. Jesus' defeat of death signifies atonement for the sins of Adam, the first "gardener." God's original intent was to have a relationship with humanity and to walk in the "garden in the cool of the day." Eden could even be appropriately defined as the heart of God. So God's initial placement of humanity was in the heart of God.

Adams rebellion ejected us from the Garden of Eden and Jesus' sacrifice brings us back into the heart of God. If we think about Jesus as a gardener the parables take on a whole new depth. His crucifixion in a garden, burial in a garden, and resurrection in a garden, all take on much deeper meaning. Jesus restores us and invites us to participate in the process of gardening. He calls us to change the world around us and to bear fruit. Are you ready to prepare the soil for dispersal of good seeds? The harvest is plentiful but the workers are few so let's grab our tools and partner with the gardener so we can take part in the crop. We have work to do, but our God is faithful.

ABOUT THE AUTHOR

Stan Lake has had a life long love of all things wild. He always has some sort of critter with him and never grew out of playing in the creeks and swamps. Stan is a native of Trinity, N.C. and currently lives in Bethania N.C. with his wife Jessica and their many animal friends. He has written and self published several children's books and he hosts and produces a DVD series about animals called "Catching Creation." He currently travels as a public speaker blending evangelism and conservation with live animals. He travels as a messenger reminding believers and unbelievers alike about the glory of God and the responsibility we have for both humanity and our responsibility as stewards of the planet we've been entrusted with. Stan is a licensed pastor and graduated from the School of Urban Missions Bible College. He is an Army combat veteran of Operation Iraqi Freedom. For more information about Stan and his adventures please visit www.CatchingCreation.com.

CHECK OUT STAN LAKE'S CATCHING CREATION DVDS...

... AND FOR YOUR YOUNG READER, HIS CHILDREN'S BOOKS

Made in the USA
Middletown, DE
28 July 2018